SO-CPU-106

God is in the Night

written by Connie Abrams

illustrated by Kathryn Hutton

©1984, The STANDARD PUBLISHING Company, Cincinnati, Ohio
Division of STANDEX INTERNATIONAL Corporation. Printed in U.S.A.

Bedtime is always a good time at Karen's
house.
Daddy reads the Bible and Mother tells
Karen one of her favorite Bible stories.

After the story one night, Karen looked
    out the window into the dark sky.
The moon was big and round.
The stars were brightly shining.
Everything else was dark.

"Mother," Karen asked, "what is in the
    night?"
"The world is like a big, big ball," Mother
    answered.
"When it's dark at our house, it's daytime
    on the other side of the world.

"At night when you are in your bed
  sleeping, the little children in China
  are playing games.
It is morning over there!

"Policemen keep our city safe at night,"
   Mother said.
"And firemen are awake to put out fires.

"Doctors and nurses in the hospitals care for the people who are sick or hurt in the night.

"Some people need to travel at night, so big airplanes fly across the dark sky. They land at brightly lighted airports. Cars go down the highway with their headlights on."

Karen and Mother listened to a long, fast
   train rumble down the track.
"Too-oo-ot! Too-oo-ot!" it whistled as it
   passed by.
"The engineer shines the train's big light
   in the night," Mother said.

"Some of the animals lie down to rest
and sleep in the night," Mother said.

"Other animals come out of the forest
when it's dark to find the food God has
made for them.

"Best of all," said Mother, "God is in the
    night."

Karen looked up into the night sky, "I see the moon and a million stars!" she said.

"How did they get up there so high?"

"God put them there," said Mother.
"In the beginning of time, God made the
 world.
He made the sun for the daytime and He
 made the moon and stars for the
 nighttime."

Karen wished it could be daytime all of the time.

"Why does it have to get dark?" she asked.

"God planned it that way," Mother said.

"God made the night so your body can rest and grow strong.
God knew that Karen's arms and legs and fingers and toes would get tired from running and playing all day."

"Doesn't God get tired, too?" asked
    Karen.
"No, Karen," Mother said. "The Bible
    tells us that God never gets tired and
    He never goes to sleep.

"When you and Daddy and I are sound
  asleep," said Mother, "God is still
  awake.
He sees all the people on the daytime
  side of the world.
He sees all the people on the nighttime
  side of the world."

"He watches over all of the forest animals and all of the farm animals.
He sees the firemen, the policemen, the doctors and the nurses as they work.
God watches over all the people who love Him and He takes good care of them.
God is caring for us right now."

"Can God see me when the light is out and my room is dark?" asked Karen.
"Yes," Mother answered.
"God sees you all the time, even if you hide from everyone else you know.

"Would you like to thank God for taking good care of you?" Mother asked.

Karen prayed, "Thank You, God, for the
  day.
Thank You for the nighttime, too.
Thank You for watching over me while I
  sleep. Amen."

Karen climbed into bed and snuggled
   close to her doll.
Mother switched off the light, but Karen
   wasn't afraid.
She knew that God could see in the dark
   and He was caring for her.

The next thing Karen knew, it was day.
And God was there, too.